How Toys Work

Ramps and Wedges

Siân Smith

www.raintreepublishers.co.uk
Visit our website to find out
more information about
Raintree books.

To order:
☎ Phone 0845 6044371
🖹 Fax +44 (0) 1865 312263
🖳 Email myorders@raintreepublishers.co.uk

Customers from outside the UK please telephone +44 1865 312262

Raintree is an imprint of Capstone Global Library Limited,
a company incorporated in England and Wales having its
registered office at 7 Pilgrim Street, London, EC4V 6LB
– Registered company number: 6695582

Text © Capstone Global Library Limited 2013
First published in hardback in 2013
First published in paperback in 2014
The moral rights of the proprietor have been asserted.

Edited by Dan Nunn, Rebecca Rissman, and Sian Smith
Designed by Joanna Hinton-Malivoire
Picture research by Mica Brancic
Production by Victoria Fitzgerald
Originated by Capstone Global Library Ltd
Printed in China

ISBN 978 1 4062 3800 6 (hardback)
16 15 14 13 12
10 9 8 7 6 5 4 3 2 1

ISBN 978 1 4062 3807 5 (paperback)
17 16 15 14 13
10 9 8 7 6 5 4 3 2 1

British Library Cataloguing in Publication Data
Smith, Sian.
    Ramps and wedges. -- (How toys work)
    1. Inclined planes--Juvenile literature.
    I. Title II. Series
    621.8'11-dc22

Acknowledgements
The author and publisher are grateful to the following for permission
to reproduce copyright material: © Capstone Publishers pp. 5, 6, 8,
9, 10, 11, 12, 13, 15, 16, 20, 21, 23 middle bottom (Karon Dubke);
Shutterstock pp.4 (© aquariagirl1970), 4 (© charles taylor), 4 (© Fesus
Robert), 4 (© Phiseksit), 7 (© LIN, CHUN-TSO), 18 (© joingate), 19
(© Mike Flippo), 17 inset (© Daniel Taeger), 17 main (© SeDmi), 22
bottom left (© Mark Yuill), 22 bottom right (© Jiri Vaclavek), 22 top left
(© c.byatt-norman), 22 top right (© macka), 22 middle top (© sarah2),
23 top (© SeDmi).

Cover photograph of a skater reproduced with permission of Getty
Images (Photonica/Connor Walberg). Back cover photograph of a toy
car on a ramp reproduced with permission of © Capstone Publishers
(Karon Dubke).

We would like to thank David Harrison, Nancy Harris, Dee Reid, and
Diana Bentley for their assistance in the preparation of this book.

Every effort has been made to contact copyright holders of material
reproduced in this book. Any omissions will be rectified in subsequent
printings if notice is given to the publisher.

Contents

Different toys

There are many different kinds
of toys.

Toys work in different ways.

Ramps

ramp

Some toys use ramps.

hillside

A ramp is like a hillside.

high place

low place

A ramp joins a high place and a low place.

Things can move up or down ramps.

Things can move slowly when they are pushed up a ramp.

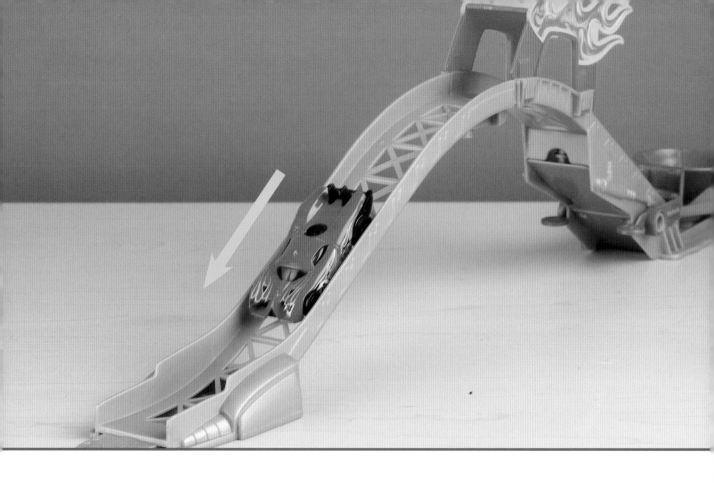

Things can move quickly when they are pushed down a ramp.

ramp

This marble run is a ramp.

This slide is a ramp.

Wedges

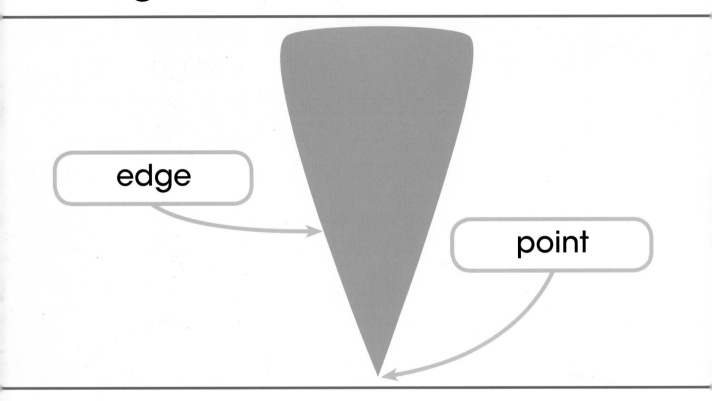

edge

point

A wedge has a sharp edge or point.

wedge

We can push wedges into things.

Wedges can stop things from moving.

wedge

Wedges can cut things apart.

wedge

The end of this spade is a wedge.

It pushes the sand apart.

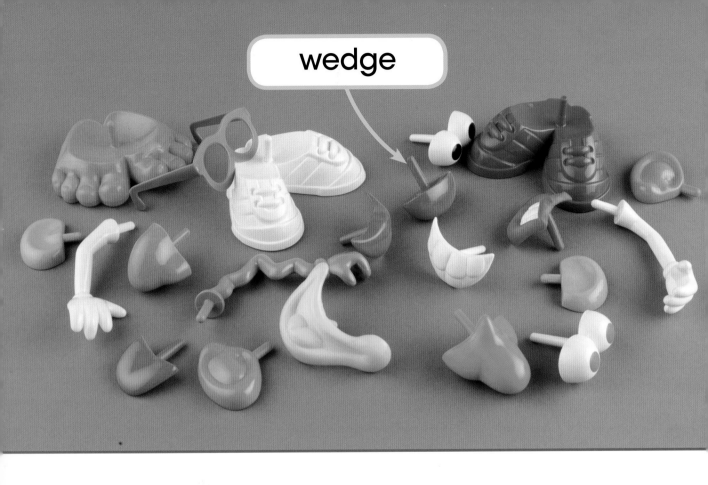

wedge

These toys have wedges.

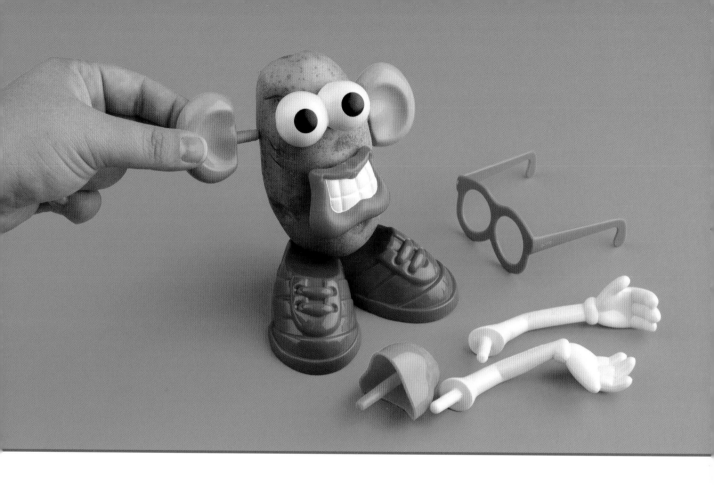

You push them into the potato.

Quiz

a

b

c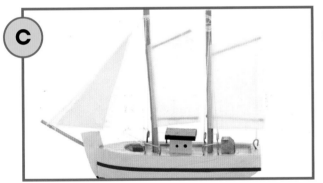

d

Which one of these toys uses a wedge to work?

Answer on page 24

Picture glossary

 **edge** the side of something. Some edges can be sharp.

 **point** a sharp end. The end of a dart is a point.

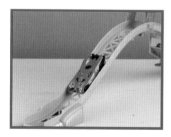 **ramp** a ramp is like a slope. It joins a high place and a low place.

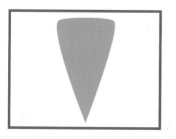 **wedge** piece of hard material with a sharp edge or point

8/13

Index

Answer to question on page 22:
Toy b uses a wedge to work. A nail is a wedge.

Notes for parents and teachers

Introduce ramps
Show an example of a simple ramp. Explain that a ramp is like a slope that connects a low place and a high place. (Ramps are also called inclined planes.) It is easier to move something heavy from a low place to a high place if you use a ramp. Help the children to design and carry out an investigation using ramps. For example investigate how far a toy car will travel if given a small push or big push down a ramp, or how changing the steepness of the ramp affects the distance it travels.

Introduce wedges
Show the children an example of a wedge, for instance a plastic knife. Explain that wedges have at least one slanting side that ends in a sharp edge. We push wedges into things to split them apart. Knives, forks, axes, and scissor blades are examples of wedges. We also sometimes use wedges to keep two things separate and stop them from moving.

Follow up activities
Take the children on a trip around a school or the home to find as many examples of ramps and wedges as you can. List, draw, or take photos of the examples you find. For more advanced work on simple machines, children can work with an adult to discuss and play the games at: www.edheads.org/activities/simple-machines